HISTORY JOURNEYS

A Tudor Journey

Philip Steele

HODDER
Wayland

an imprint of Hodder Children's Books

Produced for Hodder Wayland by
Discovery Books Ltd
Unit 3, 37 Watling Street, Leintwardine, Shropshire SY7 0LW, England

First published in 2003 by Hodder Wayland, an imprint of
Hodder Children's Books

British Library Cataloguing in Publication Data
Steele, Philip, 1948-
A Tudor journey. - (History journeys)
1. Transportation - Great Britain - History - 16th century -
Juvenile literature 2. Great Britain - History - Tudors,
1485-1603 - Juvenile literature
I. Title
388'.0941'09031

0 7502 3961 1

Printed and bound by G.Canale & C. S.p.A. - Borgaro T.se - Italy

Designer: Ian Winton
Editor: Rebecca Hunter
Illustrations: Mark Bergin

Hodder Children's Books would like to thank the following
for the loan of their material:

Bodleian Library: page 23; **The Bridgeman Art Library**: *cover*; **British Library**:
page 29; **Discovery Picture Library**: page 19 (both); **Hulton Archive**: page 5, 7
(bottom), 8, 9 (bottom), 11 (bottom), 12, 18, 20, 21, 22, 26; **Mary Evans Picture
Library**: page 4, 7 (top), 9 (top), 13, 15, (top), 16, 17, 24, 27; **Mary Rose Trust**: page
15 (bottom); **National Trust**: page 28; **Shakespeare's Globe**: page 25.

Hodder Children's Books
A division of Hodder Headline Limited
338 Euston Road
London NW1 3BH

CONTENTS

CITY OF WOOL   4

ON THE ROAD   6

FIELDS AND VILLAGES   8

COMPANY OF BEGGARS   10

HIGH AND LOW   12

A NIGHT AT THE INN   14

CITY OF LONDON   16

PALACES AND POWER   18

CHURCH BELLS   20

SCHOOL HOUSE   22

THE PLAYERS   24

A SHIP COMES IN   26

JOURNEY'S END   28

TIMELINE   30

GLOSSARY   31

FURTHER READING   31

INDEX   32

CITY OF WOOL

It is the year 1587. Jack Tallow is a servant of William Stimpson, a merchant in the Norwich wool trade. 'I have a job for you, Jack', says Master Stimpson one day. 'A ship is due to arrive in London from the Netherlands, bearing important papers. I need you to ride south and bring them back here to me.'

During the reign of Elizabeth I, England became a powerful nation.

In 1587, Queen Elizabeth I was on the throne of England. She was the grand-daughter of Henry VII, the first Tudor king, and the daughter of Henry VIII. Elizabeth had visited Norwich nine years earlier. It was a centre of the trade in woollen cloth and one of the biggest cities in the country.

In those days, cloth was manufactured by hand. Sheep were shorn with iron shears. The wool was carded (combed into strands), spun into yarn with a spinning wheel and woven on a loom. The cloth then needed fulling (cleaning and thickening) and dyeing. Bales of the finished cloth were exported all over Europe, by land and sea.

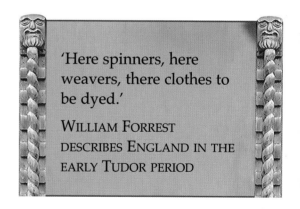

Cloth merchants, or 'clothiers' were some of the wealthiest businessmen in Europe at this time. This merchant of the 1550s is checking the value of stock in his warehouse.

The wool trade did have its ups and downs in Tudor times, but it was booming during the later years of Elizabeth I's reign. After 1565, Dutch refugees began to settle in Norwich. The newcomers, known as the 'Strangers', were skilled textile workers, who trained local people in their methods.

'Here spinners, here weavers, there clothes to be dyed.'

WILLIAM FORREST DESCRIBES ENGLAND IN THE EARLY TUDOR PERIOD

● The population of England and Wales was rising rapidly at this time. By the end of the Tudor period it had reached 5 million – about the same as that of Scotland today.

● The wool city of Norwich, in Norfolk, had a population of about 17,000. Its high city walls enclosed an area of about 260 hectares (665 acres).

ON THE ROAD

Jack is given a purse of silver coins to cover the cost of his food and lodgings on the journey. That night, he cannot sleep. He has never left Norwich in his life. He rises before dawn. His wife Anne gives him a kiss, and some bread for the journey. 'Be off with you,' she laughs, but his little daughter Alice weeps as he rides away.

This is the route Jack Tallow might have followed to London. The roads of Tudor England were mapped by Christopher Saxton in 1579.

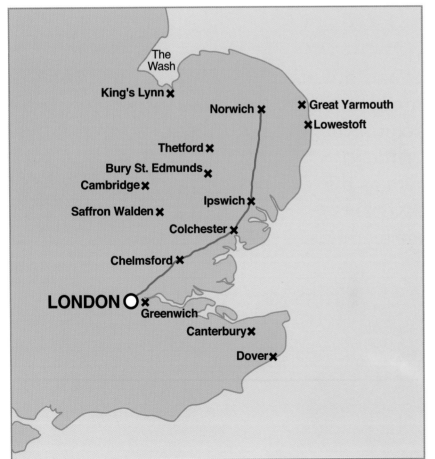

British roads had been paved in Roman times, but by the reign of Queen Elizabeth I they had become little better than cart tracks. In places they were crossed by streams and rivers, which a horseback rider had to ford. By law, each parish was supposed to organize teams of villagers to repair bridges and roads, but even so these were often full of wheel ruts and puddles. Some potholes were deep enough to drown in.

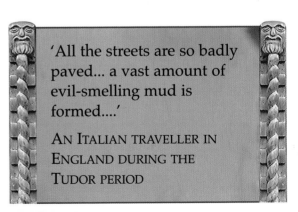

'All the streets are so badly paved... a vast amount of evil-smelling mud is formed....'

AN ITALIAN TRAVELLER IN ENGLAND DURING THE TUDOR PERIOD

- A horseback rider could hope to travel about 50 kilometres a day.

- Royal messengers used relays of horses, picking up fresh mounts from inns along the road.

- Signposts and milestones were not yet used to show routes and distances, so it was easy to get lost.

- Each year, a parish had to choose a surveyor of roads and bridges. His job was to organize upkeep and repair. He often improved the road to his own house — and then ignored the rest.

A man and his wife travel to market. Travelling two-up was uncomfortable, even for a short journey.

Most people travelled on foot or horseback. A royal messenger might gallop by at speed, but a villager would plod along on a slow, old farm horse, with his wife sitting up behind him. Proper horse-drawn coaches were not widely used in England before the 1550s. Even after this time they had no springs and gave a very bumpy ride. Curtains at the side offered a little protection from wind and rain.

Big wooden wagons were used to carry the heaviest goods. Some were hauled by teams of four or more horses. Lighter baggage was carried on packhorses or mules.

FIELDS AND VILLAGES

As the sun comes up, Jack's spirits begin to rise. He passes men, women and children labouring in the fields. Jack passes through a village and bids good day to one and all. However at the next town he curses, for his horse loses a shoe. A boy points him to the smithy.

The enclosure of land caused great hardship. In 1549 an army of 16,000 rebels led by Thomas Kett slaughtered 20,000 sheep in Norfolk, as a protest.

During the reign of Elizabeth I, eight out of every 10 people in England and Wales lived and worked in the countryside. Today it is just one out of every 10. The Tudor countryside still had large areas of natural woodland. Many fields were still open strips of common land that peasants were allowed to farm. But during Tudor times many others were enclosed by hedgerows and fences, to be grazed by sheep. This made the landowners wealthy but it took away pasture from many poor villagers.

Blacksmiths worked in the forge, melting, shaping and hammering iron. They shoed horses and made and repaired farm equipment and tools.

Barley, oats, wheat and rye were widely grown. Seed was scattered by hand. The crops were reaped with sickles, stacked in sheaves and then threshed. Both windmills and watermills were used for grinding the grain into flour. New crops were beginning to be introduced from recently discovered lands in the Americas. Potatoes were first grown in Ireland in 1586. Beehives made of straw were kept in cottage gardens and farms. Honey was normally used for sweetening foods, because sugar was very expensive.

After the 1560s, lots of new houses were built in country villages and towns. Many were timber-framed dwellings, with oak beams and plaster. They belonged to the wealthy middle classes. In some regions, houses were built of local stone. Grand houses were of stone or bricks. Poor people lived in tiny single-storey cottages, often with just one smoke-filled room and an earthen floor.

In the 1500s, farmers relied on horses, oxen or human muscle power to work the land.

COMPANY OF BEGGARS

As evening falls, Jack passes through a wood. Ahead he sees ruffians, armed with sticks. When they realize he is a servant rather than some wealthy lord, they call off their dogs. They offer him a place by their fire and some rabbit stew. Jack accepts – glad that he has already hidden his money in his boots.

The roads were not safe. Desperately poor people, beggars and vagabonds wandered the countryside in gangs and invaded the towns. Many of them were violent. Among them were unemployed servants, former soldiers, or farmworkers who had been forced from the land by enclosures or high rents. Robbers and cutpurses lay in wait for rich travellers. They had their own slang, calling their victims 'conies' (rabbits).

Two beggars are tied together and whipped out of town. At least they have escaped the gallows – for the time being.

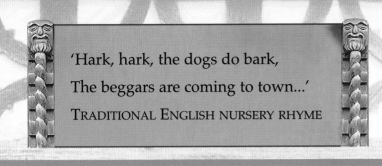

'Hark, hark, the dogs do bark,
The beggars are coming to town...'
TRADITIONAL ENGLISH NURSERY RHYME

There was no police force. Each parish paid for a watchman to keep an eye on public order. Even the smallest crimes were punished harshly. A sheep thief could be hanged from the public gallows. Beggars and vagabonds were often punished by being tied to the back of a cart and whipped through the streets. Having no income or home was a crime, unless you were too old or sick to work.

The watchman was protected by his dog and carried a wooden staff. He called out the time of day as he walked through the streets.

- In the days of Henry VII, the poor and sick were cared for and given food by monks and nuns in monasteries and convents.

- After 1536 Henry VIII closed the monasteries down, so many poor people took to the road.

- In 1570 there were said to be 2,000 beggars in the city of Norwich alone. They were accused of being wasteful trouble-makers.

- In 1598 a new Poor Law was brought in. People with no income were now given shelter, but were expected to work for the parish in return.

Criminals were often locked into wooden frames called stocks and pillories (below). The public jeered or pelted them with rubbish.

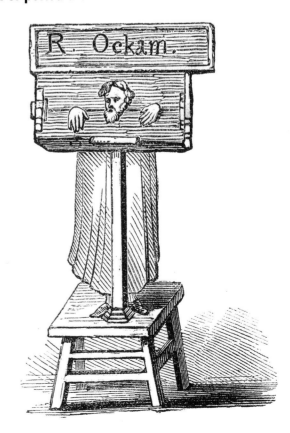

R. Ockam.

11

HIGH AND LOW

Jack leaves his companions snoring and rides off at dawn. At noon he comes across a coach with one wheel stuck in a rut. Beside it stands a fine lady. Jack helps her coachman free the wheel and warns him of the rogues in the wood. Jack is given a coin for his troubles.

All Tudor society travelled the highway. Knights, lords and ladies from the royal court could be seen out riding. They wore the most expensive cloth and fine woollen cloaks. The rich travelled in style, sometimes with their own armed guards and long trains of packhorses.

Royal guests expected to be lavishly entertained with picnics, pageants and hunts. It was a costly affair.

Queen Elizabeth I herself travelled by road, visiting towns in many parts of the kingdom. Many courtiers and servants travelled with her on these royal tours, or progresses. A progress might include as many as 400 wagons and coaches and 2,400 packhorses and riding horses. The queen stayed at grand country houses on the way.

There were other travellers on the road. Yeomen (land-owning farmers) would ride on horseback, whilst carpenters and stonemasons trudged from one building site to another. Country women herded cackling geese to market and pedlars walked from village to village selling ribbons, pins, toys and spoons from their packs.

A country woman, riding into town on an old horse, is greeted by her friends, who are gutting fish for sale at the market.

- Queen Elizabeth I had an income of up to £300,000 per year. However she had to meet many public costs that today would be paid for by the government.

- A yeoman farmer could hope for an income of £300 to £500 a year.

- Labourers and workers in the wool trade could expect to earn between just four and six pence a day.

A NIGHT AT THE INN

Clouds darken the sky and rain begins to fall. Jack decides that tonight he will sleep in an inn. He rides into the cobbled yard of *The Boar's Head*. There he has a supper of bacon and ale and warms himself by the fire, before falling asleep in a candle-lit loft, over the stables.

Many Tudor inns are still standing today. The Feathers at Ludlow, in Shropshire, was built in 1603.

Many well-known inn names date back to Tudor times. Some, such as *The Woolpack*, show that they were originally linked to the textile trade. The inn's name was pictured on boldly painted signs or flags.

A Tudor inn offered a warm welcome for the weary traveller. Around the blazing fire there might be gentlemen, farmers and carters, serving wenches, rogues, fiddlers and singers. Wealthy guests enjoyed rooms with comfortable beds, but travellers' servants could expect a lumpy, straw-filled mattress, full of fleas. In the stables, the ostler would water and feed the horses.

At taverns and inns, guests ate with their fingers, spoons, or with their own pocket knives. Table forks were still very rare.

Meals could be served to small groups in private rooms, or else at the common table. Food might include bread and cheese, salted herrings, hares, venison pies, brawn, chicken, lamb or beef roasted on the spit. There was no refrigeration, so meat had to be preserved by smoking or salting.

Beer, cider or perry were the favourite drinks in country inns, although wine was popular in city taverns. William Harrison, writing in 1577, records the import into England of 56 types of French wine and 30 other types from Italy, Greece, Spain and the Canary Islands. It was during the Tudor period that inns and taverns (pubs) first had to be officially licensed.

Inns were not just places for travellers to stay. They were somewhere to do business or to be entertained. Travelling companies of actors often performed plays in inn yards.

Mugs made of pottery or pewter (a mixture of tin and lead) were used for drinking in Tudor inns.

CITY OF LONDON

By the fourth day, Jack's road becomes busier, with horses and carts taking provisions into London, and other supplies out. At last Jack sees the city walls and finally he gazes up in wonder at the great square tower of St Paul's Cathedral.

In Tudor times, London was much smaller than it is today. It was surrounded by green fields, farms and windmills. Most areas that we think of as part of London today, such as Chelsea, Putney or Hammersmith, were still peaceful little villages.

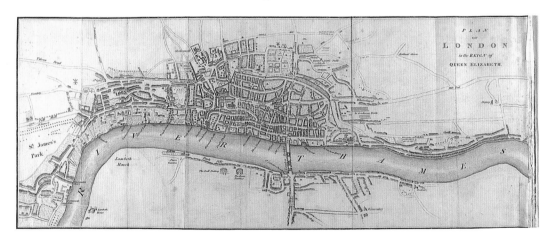

By about 1580, London was beginning to spread westwards along the banks of the River Thames. It was one of Europe's larger cities.

Inside the city walls, it was less peaceful. Between 1550 and 1600, the population of London grew from about 100,000 to 200,000. There were shopkeepers and street sellers shouting out their wares, pickpockets, housewives, apprentice boys and water carriers. The narrow streets smelt foul, for pails of dirty water and human waste were slopped out into open gutters.

London Bridge was built of stone and was topped by houses and shops on either side. It was here that the heads of traitors who had been executed were displayed to the public.

Most buildings were tall and timber-framed. Creaking wooden signs with painted designs swung from shops and taverns. There were also grand buildings in stone, such as a new merchants' centre called the Royal Exchange. London still had only one bridge across the River Thames, which crossed from the city to Southwark, on the south bank.

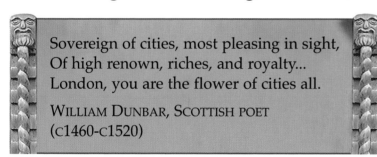

Sovereign of cities, most pleasing in sight,
Of high renown, riches, and royalty...
London, you are the flower of cities all.

WILLIAM DUNBAR, SCOTTISH POET
(c1460-c1520)

- In Tudor times, fields really did stretch northwards from the church of St Martin's-in-the-Fields – which today lies in one of the busiest parts of the city.

- Other names which survive today include Bishopsgate, Moorgate and Ludgate, which were all gates in the old city walls.

- The old St Paul's Cathedral had a high spire, which was destroyed by lightning in 1561. The whole building was lost in the Great Fire of London in 1666, and had to be rebuilt.

PALACES AND POWER

Jack finds lodgings with his master's cousin, Sir Francis Moreton, who owns a large house to the west. The ship is not due to arrive for a couple of days, so Jack has time on his hands. He visits Westminster, hoping for a glimpse of the Queen as she leaves the palace of Whitehall.

Queen Elizabeth I liked to be surrounded by a glittering court and to be the centre of attention at all times. She was pale-faced with red hair and owned over 1,000 dresses.

The fine palace at Hampton Court, on the banks of the River Thames, was given to King Henry VIII in 1529. It can still be visited today.

Elizabeth I's chief palace was at Whitehall, between Westminster Abbey and Charing Cross. It was one of Europe's biggest city palaces, covering 9 hectares (23 acres). The Queen also travelled by boat to riverside palaces at Greenwich, Richmond and Hampton Court, and hunted in the grounds of Nonsuch Palace, in Surrey. Most of the great Tudor palaces were built in the reign of Henry VIII. They were surrounded by gardens with hedges of yew and lavender.

Enemies of the state were imprisoned in the riverside fortress of the Tower of London. The 'yeoman warders' who look after the Tower still wear Tudor dress today.

The Tudor kings and queens held great personal power. They were advised by chosen officials called privy councillors. Royal power was supposed to be limited by law and by parliament, but parliament could only be called by the Queen. Queen Elizabeth I called parliament to meet at Westminster only 13 times during her long reign. Parliament had two sections, called 'houses'. The House of Lords had 90 or so members, who represented the nobles. The House of Commons had over 400 members, who represented other powerful groups such as knights and country gentlemen, wealthy merchants and lawyers. No one represented the poor. There were no political parties and most ordinary people could not vote.

This coat-of-arms was an emblem of royal power. ER stood for Elizabeth Regina (the Latin word for 'Queen').

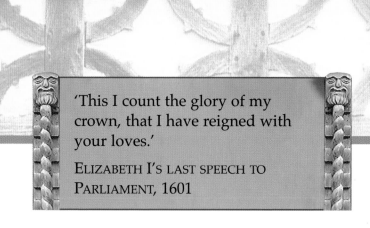

CHURCH BELLS

Jack Tallow has never seen so many churches as in London, and the ringing of their bells wakes him early on Sunday morning. He walks to a small church and the familiar words of the prayers remind him of Sundays at home in Norwich.

During the reign of Queen Elizabeth I, everyone had to go to church by law, or else be fined twelve pence. In London, long sermons were preached in the open air in the churchyard of old St Paul's Cathedral.

In Tudor times, the only high-rise buildings were churches, which had soaring spires and towers. This picture shows the London skyline 13 years after the death of Queen Elizabeth I.

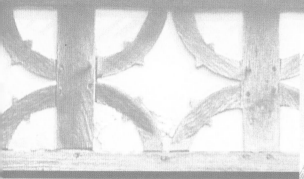

Holding the wrong religious beliefs could be dangerous in Tudor times. Protestant bishops Nicholas Ridley and Hugh Latimer were burnt alive in 1555, by Queen Mary I. She was a Roman Catholic.

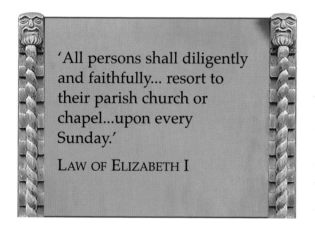

'All persons shall diligently and faithfully... resort to their parish church or chapel...upon every Sunday.'

LAW OF ELIZABETH I

The Tudor period saw bitter religious quarrels between Christians right across northern Europe, as Protestants broke away from the Roman Catholic Church. Protestants believed in simpler, plainer forms of worship using the English language rather than Latin.

Queen Elizabeth I's father, Henry VIII, had quarrelled bitterly with the Pope, the head of the Church in Rome. He had made himself head of a new English Church in 1531. His son Edward VI was a keen Protestant, but when he died and his half-sister Mary I came to the throne, she tried to bring back Roman Catholic worship. She failed and it was her half-sister Elizabeth I who brought back the English Church. Roman Catholics then had to worship secretly. Their priests sometimes hid away in secret chambers built into the house walls called 'priest holes'. Meanwhile, during the reign of Elizabeth, both Roman and English Churches were opposed by extreme Protestants called Puritans.

SCHOOL HOUSE

Early on Monday morning, Jack is asked to take the youngest son of Sir Francis Moreton to his school. They rise at five o'clock, for school started at six. Jack has never been to school himself. After seeing the teacher beat one of the pupils with a birch rod, he is glad he never went!

A pupil is thrashed with a bundle of birch twigs while others queue up to recite their Latin grammar.

Basic learning for infants was provided by the church in many villages, and also in the home. At the age of about six some boys and a few girls went to school. Poor children were expected to learn a trade.

Schools had existed since the Middle Ages, when many of them were run by monks. When Henry VIII shut down the Roman Catholic monasteries, he seized their land and wealth. Many new schools were then founded by rich Tudor merchants and supporters of the new Church.

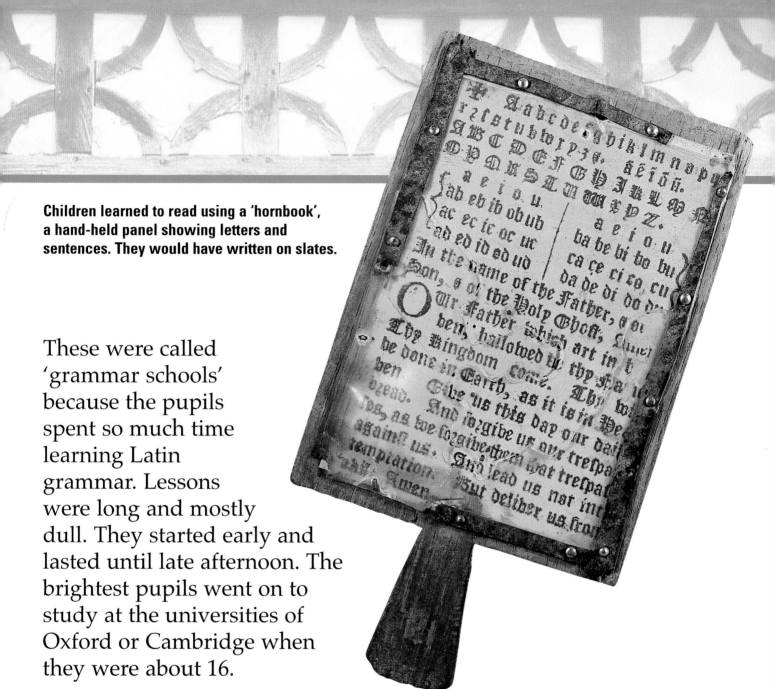

Children learned to read using a 'hornbook', a hand-held panel showing letters and sentences. They would have written on slates.

These were called 'grammar schools' because the pupils spent so much time learning Latin grammar. Lessons were long and mostly dull. They started early and lasted until late afternoon. The brightest pupils went on to study at the universities of Oxford or Cambridge when they were about 16.

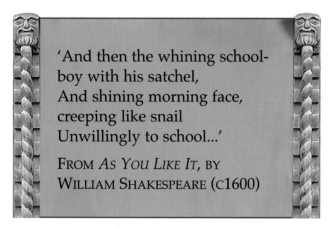

'And then the whining school-boy with his satchel,
And shining morning face, creeping like snail
Unwillingly to school...'

FROM *AS YOU LIKE IT*, BY WILLIAM SHAKESPEARE (c1600)

The children of the royal court were taught by private tutors. Queen Elizabeth I was very well educated as a young girl and was very clever. She studied Latin and ancient Greek and could speak in French, Italian and Spanish as well as English, fluently.

THE PLAYERS

On Monday afternoon, Jack has no more errands to run. He crosses London Bridge to explore the south bank of the River Thames. There he sees a big round building, flying a flag. It is the newly built Rose Theatre. Jack joins the excited crowds gathering to see a play.

Most classes of Tudor society loved to enjoy themselves with music and dancing. Public entertainments included circus acts and the cruel baiting of bulls and bears with dogs.

Many of William Shakespeare's plays were performed at London's Globe Theatre, which opened in 1598.

In early Tudor times, touring actors ('players') were thought to be no better than beggars. Many Puritans preached that plays were evil. However during the reign of Elizabeth I, theatres became more and more fashionable. Courtiers, and eventually the Queen herself, sponsored their own companies of players. The first public playhouse opened in London in 1576 and others soon followed. Tudor theatres were round buildings, open to the sky.

A new version of the old Globe theatre has been rebuilt in London. Here it stages *The Tempest*, the last play written by William Shakespeare.

The Swan Theatre, which opened in Southwark in 1596, could hold an audience of 3,000. There was little scenery or lighting. A rolling cannon ball could provide the sound effects for thunder. Acting was not thought to be a suitable job for a woman. Female parts were taken by boys.

In front of the stage was a yard, for the standing audience or 'groundlings'. They ate pies, talked and called out during performances. Richer spectators sat in three roofed galleries around the sides.

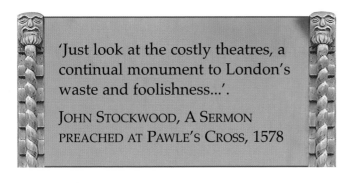

'Just look at the costly theatres, a continual monument to London's waste and foolishness...'.

JOHN STOCKWOOD, A SERMON PREACHED AT PAWLE'S CROSS, 1578

Theatres were closed at times of plague, so that the disease would not spread. Some Puritans claimed that it was the sinfulness of the players which actually caused plague in the first place.

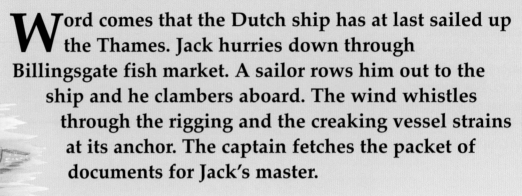

Word comes that the Dutch ship has at last sailed up the Thames. Jack hurries down through Billingsgate fish market. A sailor rows him out to the ship and he clambers aboard. The wind whistles through the rigging and the creaking vessel strains at its anchor. The captain fetches the packet of documents for Jack's master.

The Thames was very busy in Tudor times. Passengers were rowed across the river in boats called wherries. Splendid rowing barges carried the Queen and her courtiers from one palace to another. Wooden ships laden with barrels and bales sailed upstream.

The Tudor period was the greatest ever age of exploration. Small wooden ships like these set out for the Americas and Asia.

Sea-going merchant ships anchored between the Tower and London Bridge. The merchant ships used to trade across the Atlantic Ocean included the large, unwieldy galleons and the smaller caravels of Spanish and Portuguese design. By the Elizabethan age, English ships tended to be faster. All these ships were wooden three-masters, with a combination of large square sails and lateen-type triangular sails. Merchant ships carried guns and were often used in warfare.

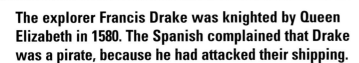

The explorer Francis Drake was knighted by Queen Elizabeth in 1580. The Spanish complained that Drake was a pirate, because he had attacked their shipping.

The great exploring nations of the 1500s and 1600s were Spain, Portugal, France, England and the Netherlands. English seafarers traded, founded settlements in distant lands and attacked the ships of England's enemies. After 1562 some also transported slaves between Africa and the Americas, a trade in human misery.

Successful sea captains included John Hawkins, Francis Drake and Walter Raleigh, all of them born in Devon. Drake sailed around the world in the years 1577-80.

- A typical merchant ship from the Port of London had a crew of 50 or so men and could carry up to 250 tonnes of cargo.

- The biggest merchant ships might be 600 tonners, with a crew of over 200.

- Shipwrecks were common in the 1500s. The *Tobie*, a 250 tonne burthen, was wrecked in a storm off Morocco in 1593. Thirty-eight members of the crew drowned and the rest were captured by the Moors.

- Sir Walter Raleigh named part of North America 'Virginia', after Elizabeth I. She was known as the 'Virgin Queen', because she was unmarried.

JOURNEY'S END

Jack gallops back north in haste. He stops briefly at a wayside fair, where he buys a doll for little Alice. In Norwich he delivers the documents to his master, who is well pleased. 'I have seen the Queen and the city,' he tells his wife, 'but now I am come home, and here will I stay.'

Rich girls might have fine dolls like the one below. Dolls bought from fairs or pedlars were much simpler.

A gift brought home from a country fair was called a fairing. Children's presents might include simple wooden dolls, toy animals, hobbyhorses or sweets.

Fairs often centred upon markets where horses or cattle were traded, or where labourers were hired by their masters. Many fairs were held on public holidays and were accompanied by all sorts of celebrations. There might be pageants, trials of strength and sports such as 'kayles' (ninepins, a form of bowling). Country people loved to dance, men and women joining hands in a large circle.

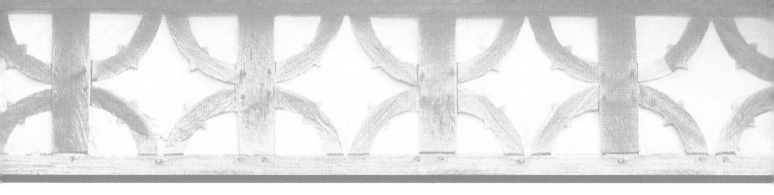

The Tudor period lasted from 1485 to 1603, when the ageing Queen Elizabeth I died. King James VI of Scotland then became also King James I of England. In the years that followed, the Puritans became more powerful and simple pleasures such as dancing were frowned upon. Many remembered the reign of Elizabeth I, for all its poverty, rebellions and executions, as a time of great happiness.

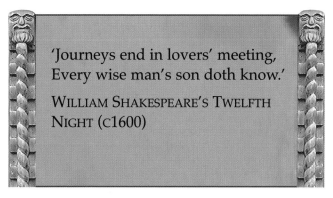

'Journeys end in lovers' meeting,
Every wise man's son doth know.'

WILLIAM SHAKESPEARE'S TWELFTH NIGHT (c1600)

Queen Elizabeth I's funeral took place in London on 28 April 1603. She was buried in Westminster Abbey.

TIMELINE

1485 — The end of the Wars of the Roses. Henry VII comes to the throne, first of the Tudors.

1509 — Henry VIII becomes king. He marries Catherine of Aragon, the first of six wives.

1513 — England defeats Scotland at the Battle of Flodden Field. King James IV of Scotland is killed.

1515 — Hampton Court palace is built.

1534 — Henry VIII breaks ties with the Roman Catholic Church.

1536 — Henry VIII dissolves (closes down) monasteries.

1536-37 — Rebellion: the 'Pilgrimage of Grace'

1536-42 — Acts of Union between England and Wales.

1545 — A new warship called the *Mary Rose* sinks in the English Channel.

1547 — Protestant Edward VI becomes king, aged 10.

1549 — Robert Kett's rebellion in Norfolk.

1550 — Population of London about 100,000.

1553 — Attempt to make Lady Jane Grey queen fails after 9 days. Catholic Mary I becomes queen.

1554 — Mary I marries King Philip II of Spain.

1558 — Elizabeth I becomes queen.

1559 — The Church of England is established.

1576 — The first commercial theatre opens in London at Shoreditch.

1579 — Christopher Saxton maps England and Wales.

1580 — Francis Drake becomes the first Englishman to sail around the world.

1585 — Walter Raleigh's first attempt to found a colony at Virginia in North America.

1586 — Potatoes, an American crop, first grown in Ireland.

c1587 — Playwright William Shakespeare arrives in London.

1587 — Elizabeth I orders the execution of her cousin Mary, Queen of Scots, exiled in England.

1588 — Spain sends an Armada (war fleet) but fails to invade England.

1595-1601 — Rebellion against English rule in Ireland.

1598 — Poor Law offers shelter to those with no income.

1600 — Population of London about 200,000.

1601 — Elizabeth I makes her last speech to Parliament.

1603 — Death of Elizabeth I, last of the Tudors. James VI of Scotland, a member of the Stuart family, becomes ruler of England too, as James I.

GLOSSARY

apprentice — A boy or teenager who is learning a craft or trade.

burthen — The measurement of the load a ship can carry.

card — To untangle woollen fleece with a comb, so that it can be spun into yarn.

civil war — A conflict between two sides within the same country, such as the Wars of the Roses.

courtier — One of the group of lords, ladies and knights who attend upon a king or queen.

cutpurse — Someone who attacks people and steals their money, a 'mugger'.

export — (1) A product sent from a country to be sold abroad. (2) To send products abroad to be sold.

ford — (1) A place where a stream or river flows over a road, shallow enough to cross. (2) To cross over such a place.

full — To thicken up woven cloth, by washing and by treating with a kind of clay called fuller's earth, which removes grease from the wool.

gallows — A wooden frame from which people found guilty of crimes were hanged, in public.

loom — A wooden frame on which threads are interwoven to make textiles.

ostler — Someone who looks after travellers' horses at an inn.

parish — The district around a church, an area of administration in Tudor times.

Parliament — Literally, a 'talking session'. Parliaments were assemblies of people who represented regions of the country.

pedlar — A man who travelled around the countryside selling household items and trinkets from his pack.

perry — An alcoholic drink made from pears, in the same way that cider is made from apples.

Pope — The head of the Roman Catholic Church.

Privy Councillor — One of a panel of private ('privy') advisers appointed by the king or queen to carry out affairs of state.

Protestant — A Christian opposed to many of the teachings, forms of worship and customs of the Roman Catholic Church.

Puritan — Any Christian who believed in a very strict form of Protestant teaching.

reap — To cut wheat or other grain crops for the harvest.

Roman Catholic — A Christian supporting the teachings of the Church in Rome.

sheaf — Stalks of wheat or other grain crops that have been cut and bundled together.

spit — A metal rod on which meat is skewered and turned around in front of a fire, for roasting.

stonemason — A building worker skilled in cutting, shaping, polishing and fitting stone.

Stuart — (originally Stewart) (1) The name of the royal family of Scotland from 1371 to 1714, and of England from 1603 to 1714. (2) The name of the period in which they ruled.

textile — Any woven cloth.

thresh — To beat the grain from the stalks of wheat or other crops, after reaping.

Tudor — (originally Tudur) (1) A Welsh family name, that of the rulers of England and Wales between 1485 and 1603. (2) The name of the period in which the Tudors ruled.

vagabond — A vagrant or tramp, a homeless person who wanders from place to place without any income.

venison — Meat from deer.

wench — A young working-class woman in town or country, a serving girl in an inn.

wherry — (1) A light rowing boat used to ferry passengers across rivers. (2) A larger sailing barge used to transport goods.

yeoman — An independent farmer or small landowner, a member of the middle classes.

FURTHER READING

All About The Tudors, by Heather Morris, Hodder Wayland, 2001
The History Detective Investigates: *Tudor Home* (Alan Childs), *Tudor Medicine* (Richard Tames), *Tudor Theatre* (Alan Childs), *Tudor War* (Peter Hepplewhite), Hodder Wayland, 2002

INDEX

actors 15, 24, 25
America 9, 27

bear baiting 24
bee-keeping 9
beggars 10, 11
blacksmiths 8, 9
boats 26

churches 20, 21, 22
clothiers 5
coaches 7, 12
common land 8
courtiers 12
crops 9
cutpurses 10

Drake, Sir Francis 27
drink 15
dyeing 4

Edward VI 21
Elizabeth I 4, 5, 6, 8, 12, 18, 19, 21, 23, 24, 29
enclosures 8
entertainments 24, 25
exports 4, 27

fairs 28
farming 8, 9
food 15
fulling 4
funerals 29

galleons 26
Globe Theatre 24, 25
grammar schools 23
Great Fire of London 17
Greenwich 18

Hampton Court 18
hanging 10, 11
Henry VII 4, 11
Henry VIII 4, 18, 21
honey 9
horn books 23

horses 6, 7, 9, 12, 13, 16

inns 14, 15

James VI of Scotland/I of England 29

Latin 21, 23
London 4, 16, 17, 20
London Bridge 17

maps 6, 16
markets 13, 28
Mary I (Tudor) 21
merchants 4, 5, 19, 22
messengers 7
monasteries 22

Netherlands 4
Norwich 4, 5, 6, 11

ostlers 14
oxen 9

packhorses 7, 12
palaces 18
Parliament 19
pedlars 13
pillories 11
plague 25
plays 24, 25
poor, the 10, 11, 19, 22
population 5, 16
potatoes 9
priest holes 21
progresses 12
Protestants 21
punishments 10, 11, 22
Puritans 21, 24, 25, 29

Raleigh, Sir Walter 27
Richmond 18
roads 6, 10
Roman Catholics 21
Royal Exchange 17

St Martin's-in-the-Fields, London 17
St Paul's Cathedral, London 16, 17, 20
schools 22, 23
Shakespeare, William 24, 25
sheep 4
ships 4, 18, 26, 27
slave trade 27
soldiers 10
spinning 4
stocks 11

taverns 15, 17
textiles 5
Thames, River 17, 26
theatres 24, 25
timber frames 9, 14, 17
toys 28
travellers 12, 13, 14

universities 23

vagabonds 10, 11
villages 8, 9, 16, 22

wages 13
watchmen 11
watermills 9
Westminster Abbey 18, 29
Whitehall 18
windmills 9, 16
wool trade 4, 5, 13

yeomen 13